Are [you] ready [for] Art At[tack?]

Bored with your ro[om? Does it need] a makeover?

In this book you wi[ll find] funky ideas to add [...] and a few stylish to[uches to your] room. All of them a[re easy] to do and guarante[ed to brighten] up your bedroom an[d] organise your junk!

So if you're ready [to give] your room turn the [page and] have some Art At[tack fun!]

[Con]tents

[...] Brown Designer: Antony Gardner
[...]: Susie Johns Artist: Paul Gamble

HANG ON!

THE FIRST THING YOU'LL NEED IS A DOORHANGER - LEAVE A WARNING MESSAGE ON YOUR BEDROOM DOOR!

1. Trace or photocopy the doorhangers on the right hand page. Cut out the one you want.
2. Stick the doorhangers onto coloured card to give it a nice bright background.
3. Cut the doorhangers out and then colour in brightly.
4. Finally, hang on your door!

IF YOU DON'T WANT TO RUIN YOUR BOOK, DON'T CUT THEM OUT. ASK AN ADULT TO PHOTOCOPY THIS PAGE FOR YOU INSTEAD.

AND WHILE YOU'RE MAKING THEM, YOU CAN MAKE AN EXTRA ONE FOR A BROTHER OR A SISTER.

FAKE FISH!

JAZZ UP A DARK CORNER WITH A FUNNY FAKE FISH TANK. NOT ONLY WILL YOU HAVE SOME VIRTUAL PETS, YOU CAN USE IT TO STORE STUFF.

1. Take the cardboard box and carefully cut away one side. Tape one of the flaps down at the top.
2. Draw a sandy sea bottom on the box side that you cut away and stick this to the front of the box.
3. Cut another piece of card the same size as the box. Place this inside the box to make the fishy background. It should be secured in place where the top flap is stuck down. Now you should have a compartment at the back.
4. Cover the whole thing with 2 layers of papier maché and leave to dry.
5. Now you can paint it. Paint the whole thing white to cover the newspaper and leave to dry again.
6. Paint the box a nice sea blue adding darker shades of blue for shadow. Paint some fish on the background and paint the sandy piece, yellowy brown.
7. Trace the fish below onto thick card and paint. Fix them in place by sticking them to lollipop sticks and securing them to the bottom of the box.

Use your fake fish tank to store homework or stationary or anything you like!

YOU WILL NEED:

Cardboard box, card, scissors, sticky tape or glue, newspaper, PVA glue, lollipop sticks, paints.

Get Sorted

Can't find your undies in the morning? Different coloured socks? Well you need to get sorted with these...

1

Arrange your tubes on a piece of cardboard box card in the shape of a socks or pants. When you're happy with the arrangement, glue the tubes to the card and each other.

2

Leave the glue to dry, then trim all round the shape. Cut a long strip of corrugated card, the same width as the loo roll tubes and wrap it right round, taping it to the tubes as you go.

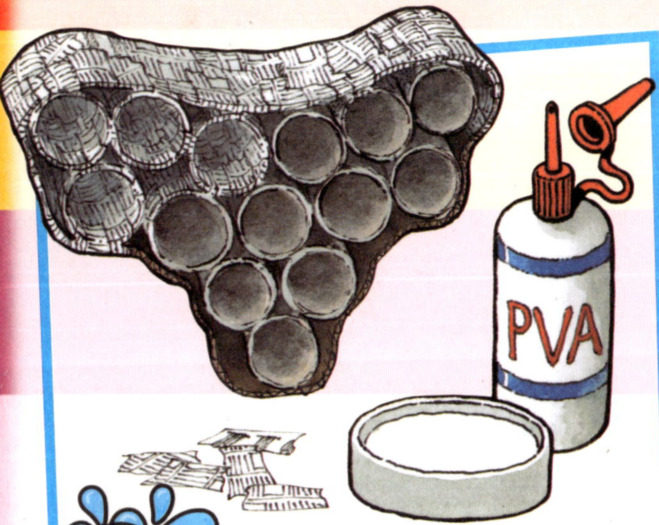

3

Now cover the whole construction with about 3 layers of papier maché. (See tips on page 26 for how to do this.) Leave them to dry.

4

Paint your models white all over then paint colourful stripes on the sock and a pretty pattern on the pants. Or paint the pants to look like sporty Y-fronts! It's up to you!

YOU WILL NEED:

Cardboard box card,
toilet rolls,
sticky tape,
newspaper,
PVA glue,
paints.

MIRROR MOTIFS

Mirror, mirror on the wall, who's the artiest of them all?

Well, you may not get an answer but you're sure to have a laugh with these hilarious mirror motifs!

You will need:

Tracing paper, thin card, scissors, felt tips, sticky tack.

Simply trace the images on to thin card or thick paper, cut them out, colour them in and stick them on your mirror! If you use sticky tack, you can move them around according to how you feel!

Remember you can photocopy the page. How about making a few for the bathroom mirror?

Head width apart
You're gorgeous!

WALL ART

TRANSFORM YOU ROOM WITH THESE 3D WALL SHAPES. TRY THESE AND THEN MAKE SOME OF YOUR OWN - THEY'RE EASY!

1

Cut basic shapes from thick card. Make them as big as you like. For the whale, you may find it easier to cut the whale shape and the water spout shape separately. For the egg, cut the outline shape then cut a small round circle for the yolk.

2

Pad out the shapes to make them more three-dimensional. Use crumpled paper or plastic carrier bags, taping them firmly in place.

3

Now cover your shapes with three layers of papier maché. Leave to dry, and then paint white. This helps to cover up the newspaper and gives a good base for any colours you are going to use.

4

Paint the splat a bright colour, with white highlights. Paint the whale blue-grey and paint the egg white and yellow!

YOU WILL NEED:

Cardboard box, sticky tape, newspaper, plastic carrier bags, PVA glue, paints.

DREAM SCREEN!

BRIGHTEN UP A BORING COMPUTER WITH THE HELP OF THIS ART-TASTIC SCREEN SURROUND!

YOU WILL NEED: Thin card, glue, pencil, scissors, felt tips, sticky tack.

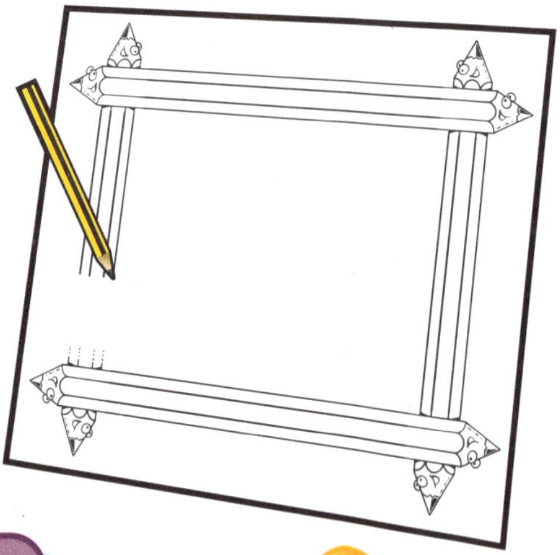

1. Measure your computer screen and mark out the size on a large piece of thin card. Start by putting the four corners in position. Trace off or photocopy the corner pencils and stick them in the corners.
2. Join up the corner pencils by drawing lines. Then cut the border out and colour it in with felt tips.
3. Trace off or photocopy all the other pieces. Stick them onto thin card, colour and cut them out.
4. Stick the pieces around the border. You can put them in any position and use as many of them as you want. (As you can see I have used the splats on the top and bottom.)

STICK THE SURROUND TO YOUR COMPUTER USING BLOBS OF STICKY TACK.

STEREO STORAGE!

Check out this sound idea for storage. This musical make is perfect for holding cds, tapes or anything!

1

Tape the flaps of the boxs closed. Then mark lines on the top corners of the box and cut away. Curve the side panels of the box around these cut edges and tape firmly in place. Cut a hole in the top of the box, just large enough to get your hand in.

2

Make two cardboard rings from scrap card and then draw around them. Cut out these circles and glue them to the rings. Glue the rings to the front of the box.

3

Now make or find a shallow box and stick a large margarine lid on the front. Stick this on the centre front of the box.

YOU WILL NEED:

Cardboard box, card, scissors, small shallow box, margarine lid, newspaper, PVA glue, paint.

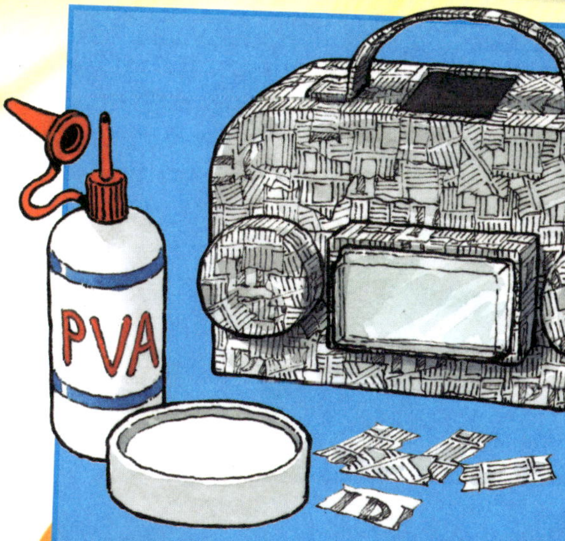

4

Cover the whole thing with 3 or 4 layers of papier maché and leave to dry.

5

Paint with bright colours. Metallic paints are particularly effective. Don't forget to add buttons and dials with a permanent black pen

DESIGN-A-LABELS!

MAKE YOUR MARK WITH THESE SUPER COOL LABELS. SIMPLY FOLLOW THE STEPS TO GET LABELLED...,

You will need:
scissors - felt tips - glue

1. Trace or photocopy the jar labels on the right hand page. If you photocopy them, you can shrink or enlarge them depending on how big your boxes or jars are.

2. Cut the labels out and then colour them in brightly. Colour the name space in a light colour so you can write in it.

3. Now stick the labels to jars, boxes or anything you want to store things in.

Make lots of labels but instead of writing your name in the space, write what you are collecting. What about stickers, football cards, jewellery, Art Attack bits, whatever?

If you don't want to ruin your book, don't cut them out. Ask an adult to photocopy this page for you instead.

Zebra Shelf

BRING SOME ANIMAL MAGIC TO YOUR ROOM WITH THIS STRIPE-TASTIC ZEBRA SHELF!

1

Cut two dividers from the shoe box lid and glue these in place inside the box.

2

From any remaining cardboard, cut a basic head shape, then wrap this with several layers of newspaper, to pad out the shape.

YOU WILL NEED:

Cardboard box, card, sticky tape, newspaper, PVA glue, black and white tissue paper, string, paints.

3

Cover the box and the head with about 3 or 4 layers of papier maché. Leave to dry. Then glue the head to one corner of the box. Leave until the glue is dry.

4

Make holes in the base of the box, and in one end of each cardboard tube, and attach the legs to the 'body'.

5

Now have fun decorating your zebra shelf. Paint it white all over - you may need two coats - then paint black stripes.

6

Make the tail by plaiting one sheet of black tissue paper and two sheets of white. Roll each sheet lengthways into a long sausage, flatten, then staple the three sheets together at one end. Plait, then bind the end with string and attach the tail to the box.

FUNKY FRAMES!

TO HIGHLIGHT SPECIAL PICTURES AND PRECIOUS PHOTOS, MAKE SOME FABULOUS FRAMES FOR BOTH THE WALL AND SIDE TABLE!

FOLLOW THE STEPS TO MAKE THE FRAMES - JUST MAKE THEM DIFFERENT SIZES IF YOU WANT THEM AS A PHOTO OR PICTURE FRAME

PHOTO FINISH!

YOU WILL NEED:

Cardboard, newspaper, sticky tape, PVA glue, paint.

PICTURE PERFECT!

1. Cut out the basic shapes from card - a circle for a football and the crown shape for the other one.
2. Cut out a rectangle in the middle big enough for your picture.
3. For the football, build up the shape by sticking balls of scrunched up newspaper on the card circle.
4. For the princess frame, roll small sausages of paper pulp (see tips on p26) into letters and stick on the backing card. Stick on other pulp shapes like little balls and stars.
5. When you're happy with both frames, cover with 3 layers of torn newspaper strips pasted on with PVA glue. Leave to dry until rock hard.
6. Paint the football white all over and then, when dry, paint black hexagons. Paint the princess frame white. When dry, paint the frame pink, leaving the letters white. Paint the stars and any other patterns you want.
7. Finally add some pictures. Stick them to the back with sticky tape.

ASK AN ADULT IF YOU CAN STICK A FRAME TO YOUR BEDROOM WALL AND THEN USE STICKY TACK.

TO MAKE IT INTO A PHOTO FRAME FOR A TABLE, CREATE A CARDBOARD STAND LIKE THIS.

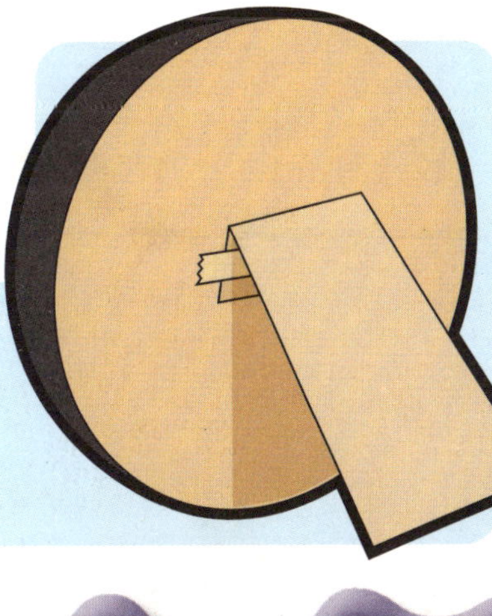

JUNK FOOD TI

HOW ABOUT THIS FOR A UNIQUE WAY TO KEEP YOUR STUFF SORTED? PERFECT FOR PENS, PENCILS, BRUSHES AND ANYTHING YOU DON'T WANT TO LOSE!

1 For the ketchup money box, start with a small plastic bottle. Cut a piece of corrugated card wide enough to wrap around the bottle and the same height. Snip the card, halfway down, along the ridges, then wrap around the bottle. Overlap the snipped tabs and tape them firmly in place.

2 Wrap a smaller strip of card around the top of the bottle and stick a round disk of card on top, with a slit cut in it. Stick a circle of card over the base of the bottle, too, to cover up any dimples or bumps.

3 For the cola can and the baked bean can, start with a cocoa tin. Wrap with a rectangle of corrugated card, cut to fit. Tape the card firmly in place.

4 To make the burger bun, cut two circles of card. Wrap a narrow piece of corrugated card around both to make an edge and stuff one with paper. For the burger itself, cut another circle of card and pad out with newspaper.

ES

YOU WILL NEED:

Plastic bottle without a lid, card, 2 cocoa tins, sticky tape, newspaper, PVA glue, paints.

5

Now cover all the items with about 3 or 4 layers of papier maché. (See tips on page 26 for how to do this.) Leave to dry.

6

Paint each piece with a coat of white paint, then add lots of colour and detail. You can copy lettering and designs from real cans of drink or bottles of ketchup, or make up your own.

HINTS AND TIPS!

Papier Maché

Make a paste from PVA glue and water. You'll find that you will need to mix the PVA glue in equal parts with water or 2 parts PVA to 1 part water to get a good consistency.

Rip up strips of paper; you can use newspaper, tissue paper or kitchen towell. Then dip the paper into the glue mixture and stick to the model usiing a brush to smooth it down.

Cover the model with a couple of layers and then leave to dry. Add another couple of layers and let dry again. The more layers you add, the stronger it will be.

Paper Pulp

To make paper pulp, just add some diluted PVA glue to a bowl of ripped kitchen towell. The paper should be wet and pliable - perfect for moulding shapes and letters.

Paints

When the 'You will need' list says 'paints,' you can use poster paints or acrylics. Both types are available in a wide range of colours, including gold and silver - though acrylics also come in glossy and metallic colours. It's your room, so choose the colours you like best!

Finishing Touches

Check out your local craft shop for glitter glue, beads and sequins to decorate existing items such as picture frames, lamp shades and mirrors or for decorating things you have made yourself, from card or papier maché.